OUTLAWS

ANN WEIL

www.raintreepublishers.co.uk

Visit our website to find out more information about **Raintree** books.

To order:
☎ Phone 44 (0) 1865 888112
🗎 Send a fax to 44 (0) 1865 314091
💻 Visit the Raintree bookshop at **www.raintreepublishers.co.uk** to browse our catalogue and order online.

First published in Great Britain by Raintree, Halley Court, Jordan Hill, Oxford OX2 8EJ, part of Harcourt Education. Raintree is a registered trademark of Harcourt Education Ltd.

Editorial: Melanie Waldron and Catherine Clarke
Design: Victoria Bevan and Bigtop
Picture Research: Hannah Taylor
Production: Julie Carter

Originated by Chroma Graphics Pte. Ltd
Printed and bound in China by Leo Paper Group

ISBN 978 1 4062 0682 1 (hardback)
12 11 10 09 08
10 9 8 7 6 5 4 3 2 1

ISBN 978 1 4062 0703 3 (paperback)
12 11 10 09 08
10 9 8 7 6 5 4 3 2 1

British Library Cataloguing in Publication Data

Weil, Ann
Outlaws. – (True stories) (Atomic)
364.1'0922
A full catalogue record for this book is available from the British Library.

Acknowledgements

The publishers would like to thank the following for permission to reproduce photographs: akg–images p. **16**; Alamy Images (Mary Evans Picture Library) p. **20**; Australian Film Commission (Working Title/The Kobal Collection/Johns, Carolyn) p. **23**; Bridgeman Art Library pp. **5** (Look and Learn/Private Collection), **13** (Private Collection/The Stapleton Collection), **15** (top) (Private Collection/Peter Newark American Pictures); Corbis (Bettmann) pp. **6** (top), **19**, **27**; CPImages p. **24**; Mary Evans Picture Library pp. **10**, **29**, **15** (bottom); Topfoto p. **9**; Topham (AP) p. **6** (bottom).

Cover photograph of 1920s to 1930s gangsters reproduced with permission of Corbis (Bettmann).

The publishers would like to thank Nancy Harris, Diana Bentley, and Dee Reid for their assistance in the preparation of this book.

Every effort has been made to contact copyright holders of any material reproduced in this book. Any omissions will be rectified in subsequent printings if notice is given to the publishers.

Disclaimer

Contents

Some words are printed in bold, **like this**. You can find out what they mean in the glossary. You can also look in the box at the bottom of the page where the word first appears.

WHAT IS AN OUTLAW?

An outlaw is a criminal – someone who lives outside the law.

Robin Hood

There have been outlaws throughout history. Some outlaws have become **legends**. Stories about them are told repeatedly, and these retellings may change the facts to create a more exciting story.

Stories about Robin Hood have been told for more than 600 years. He and his band of outlaws lived in Sherwood Forest and fought the **tyranny** of Prince John and the evil Sheriff of Nottingham.

folk hero	hero of ordinary people
legend	old story that might not be true, or a very famous person from history
tyranny	cruel leadership

Outlaw fact!

Stories about how Robin Hood stole from the rich to give to the poor made him a popular folk hero. Was Robin Hood a real person or a legend? No one knows for certain.

Bonnie playfully points a shotgun at her partner in crime, Clyde.

Bonnie and Clyde were each shot more than 50 times in this car.

BONNIE AND CLYDE

Clyde Barrow was wanted for robbery when he and Bonnie Parker met in 1930 and fell in love.

One month later he was **apprehended** and sent to jail in Texas, USA. He escaped using a gun that Bonnie had sneaked in to him. Two weeks later, Clyde was back behind bars.

Wanted: dead or alive

When Clyde was released on **parole** in 1932, he returned to crime. In 1934 he organized a jailbreak from his old prison. The hunt for Bonnie and Clyde was stepped up. Finally, police **ambushed** and shot the pair dead in their car.

Outlaw fact!

While in prison from 1930 to 1932, "Clyde turned from a schoolboy to a rattlesnake", according to another prisoner.

ambush	hide and wait to catch someone by surprise
apprehend	catch and arrest
parole	leaving prison early on the condition of good behaviour

Charles "Pretty Boy" Floyd

Charles Floyd's first known crime was in 1922, when he was 18 years old. He stole £181 in pennies from a post office.

A life of crime

Three years later, Floyd was arrested for a robbery in St. Louis, Missouri, USA. After serving three years in jail, Floyd was released on **parole**, but he continued to break the law.

Finally, Floyd was **apprehended** while robbing a bank. He was arrested and **sentenced**, but escaped on the way to prison. On 22 October 1934, he was shot and killed by FBI agents.

Outlaw fact!

In July 1934 Floyd became "Public Enemy Number One" in the United States.

sentence	punishment for a crime, usually a period of time to be spent in jail

CHARLES ARTHUR FLOYD

ALIAS "PRETTY BOY FLOYD"

Floyd earned the nickname "Pretty Boy" Floyd because of his good looks. His fresh face appeared on this wanted poster.

Highwaymen on horses robbed travellers and then galloped away.

DICK TURPIN

For hundreds of years, highwaymen were a danger throughout England, but especially in and around the city of London. Most were vicious bandits. Some, like Dick Turpin, became legends.

Stop thief!

Turpin lived in the early 1700s. He owned a butcher shop. He stole **livestock** so he would not have to pay for the meat he sold. Then, Turpin was caught stealing farm animals.

Turpin fled London and escaped to the countryside, where he joined a gang of bandits. These bandits stole and killed deer that belonged to the royal family. They also broke into houses and terrorized the owners into revealing where they hid their money and valuables. Finally the gang were tracked down. Some gang members were hanged. Turpin escaped and became a highwayman.

bandit	another word for thief, robber, or outlaw
highwayman	thief who robs travellers on the road
livestock	farm animals raised for meat, dairy, or other uses

Hanged for a horse!

One day, Turpin stole a beautiful black horse from its owner at gunpoint. The horse's owner wanted his prize horse back. He knew Turpin was the thief and alerted police.

The police found the black horse – and Turpin – at a **tavern**. There was a shootout. Turpin escaped on the horse, but was later found. He was hanged as a horse thief in York, in 1739.

Outlaw fact!

A story says that Turpin rode Black Bess, the stolen horse, 240 kilometres (150 miles) in less than 15 hours. Historians say Turpin never made this famous ride, but that a highwayman nicknamed "Swift Nick" did make a similar ride.

tavern   bar, pub, or inn

Turpin's horse Black Bess became almost as famous as he was!

BELLE STARR, THE "BANDIT QUEEN"

Myra Belle Shirley was born in 1848 in Missouri, USA. Her father came from a wealthy family, and Belle (as Myra was known) had many luxuries growing up. Then, Belle fell in love with an outlaw called Jim Reed. She married him and became an outlaw herself.

Violent life, violent death

After Reed was killed, Belle remarried. She became the leader of a gang that stole cattle and horses. After her husband Sam Starr was killed in a gunfight, Belle remarried again.

Belle was shot to death in 1889, when she was 40 years old. Her killer was never identified.

infamous   famous for bad deeds

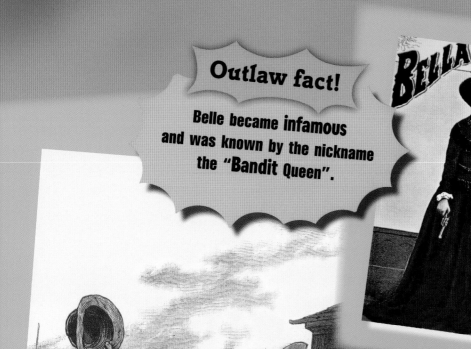

Outlaw fact!

Belle became infamous and was known by the nickname the "Bandit Queen".

BELLA STARR
THE BANDIT QUEEN
OR THE
FEMALE JESSE JAMES

Handsomely
AND
Profusely
Illustrated
PRICE
25¢

"I regard myself as a woman who has seen much of life," Belle said in a newspaper interview a year before she died.

During the 1890s, the Dalton gang robbed trains like this one.

THE DALTON GANG

The Dalton brothers started out as lawmen in the Wild West. Their older brother, Frank, was a US deputy marshal. He was killed in the line of duty in 1887.

The younger Dalton brothers followed in Frank's footsteps and also became lawmen. Then, they moved to the other side of the law. The Dalton brothers and their gang of outlaws began to rob trains.

Diving into crime

In 1891 Gratton "Grat" Dalton was **convicted** of robbery. While he was on a train taking him to jail he made a daring escape! He dived out of the window into a river, and then swam to safety.

convict — prove guilty

deputy marshal — law officer, like a sheriff

Wild West — western United States during the period of its settlement in the 1800s

The Dalton gang robbed train stations as well as trains. In one robbery, they stole everything from the station's baggage rooms. Then, they waited for the train, sitting with their guns across their laps. When the train came in, they robbed it. The train guards fired at the **bandits**. There was a gunfight during which two guards were killed, but the Dalton gang members were not injured.

Two banks too many

On 5 October 1892, the Dalton gang set out to rob two banks in their hometown on the same day. They wore fake beards, but people still recognized them. The townspeople armed themselves and got ready to shoot it out with the Daltons. The Dalton gang was outnumbered, and every member was killed or captured.

Members of the Dalton gang lay dead after a shootout in their hometown of Coffeyville, Kansas, USA.

These bushrangers are attacking riders carrying gold.

NED KELLY

Ned Kelly grew up in Australia in the mid-1800s. His father died when Ned was about 11 years old. Since his family was poor, Ned and his brother, Dan, stole to help the family survive.

Brothers in crime

After their mother remarried, Ned and his brother helped their stepfather steal horses. In 1878 a policeman went to arrest Ned's brother, Dan, for stealing horses. The policeman said that Ned had tried to kill him. Ned and Dan hid out in the **bush**, knowing that there was a reward for Ned "dead or alive".

Ned and Dan formed a gang with other **bushrangers**. Then, one day, Ned and his gang stumbled upon police camped in the bush. Knowing the police would try to shoot him on sight, Ned shot and killed the police.

bush	wild parts of Australia where few people live
bushranger	outlaw in Australia in the 1800s

After this the reward for Ned Kelly and his gang became £8,000, which would be several million pounds today!

Brave outlaw

Ned's friends helped him avoid the police for almost two years. Then, in 1880, police surrounded the Kelly gang. Ned and the other **bushrangers** wore steel armour. Ned escaped, but returned to try to rescue his friends. Eventually Ned collapsed from his wounds and was arrested. He was the only gang member to survive the gun battle.

Ned was **sentenced** to death. Some people protested his sentence, since they did not want this **folk hero** to die.

Outlaw fact!

Today, the legend of Ned Kelly is still strong in Australia and throughout the world because of books and films.

In 2003, a film of Ned Kelly's life was made starring Heath Ledger as Ned.

Boyd was Canada's "Public Enemy Number One" in the 1950s.

EDWIN BOYD

Canadian Edwin Boyd was the son of a Toronto policeman, yet he led a life of crime.

Young Boyd stole money from his relatives. At the age of 22 he robbed a petrol station. After fighting in World War II (1939–1945), he used a German gun he brought back to rob a Toronto bank.

Dressed for crime

Boyd went to jail, but then he escaped and formed a gang that became known for bold bank robberies. Boyd always wore a **fedora** and carried a gun.

In 1952 gang members shot a policeman. Boyd was not at the murder, but he still went to prison. He was finally released in 1966 and lived to be 88 years old.

fedora   stylish hat with a brim around it

Pancho Villa

Doroteo Arango was born in Mexico in 1878. He worked on a hacienda.

The story goes that one day he returned home from the fields and found that the owner of the hacienda had attacked his sister. He shot the owner and escaped into the mountains on horseback.

New outlaw, old name

Then, Arango became a cattle **rustler** and joined a gang led by an outlaw named Francisco "Pancho" Villa. After police killed this older outlaw, Arango became the gang's new leader and took the name Pancho Villa as his own.

assassinate	murder a leader
hacienda	Mexican plantation
Mexican Revolution	time of fighting between the people of Mexico and its leaders
rustler	thief who steals farm animals, usually horses or cattle

Outlaw fact!

Pancho Villa became a war hero during the **Mexican Revolution.**

Many people loved Pancho Villa (centre), but others saw him as a cruel, cold-blooded killer. He had many enemies and was **assassinated** in 1923 while driving his car.

OUTLAWS: FACT OR FICTION?

William Wallace has become a legend, but the stories about him, like the stories told about other outlaws, might be more fiction than fact.

William Wallace lived during a time when the Scottish people were fighting to free themselves from English rule. His father was killed by an English knight. Wallace wanted revenge, so he hunted and murdered the knight who had killed his father. This made him an enemy of the English king. Wallace formed an army to fight the English. He was a fearsome warrior and a skilful leader. When a Scottish knight serving the English king betrayed him, Wallace was taken to London and executed.

Was William Wallace an honourable man, forced to live outside the law by powerful enemies? Was he a hero, or just a cold-blooded killer? Some of these questions could just as easily be asked about other outlaws as well.

fiction made-up story

William Wallace (right) led the Scottish people in several battles against the English. Today, he is remembered by many as a hero.

Glossary

ambush hide and wait to catch someone by surprise

apprehend catch and arrest

assassinate murder a leader

bandit another word for thief, robber, or outlaw

bush wild parts of Australia where few people live

bushranger outlaw in Australia in the 1800s

convict prove guilty. Sentencing takes place after a person is convicted of a crime.

deputy marshal law officer, like a sheriff

fedora stylish hat with a brim around it

fiction made-up story

folk hero hero of ordinary people. Folk heroes are usually connected with a particular place or area.

hacienda Mexican plantation

highwayman thief who robs travellers on the road

infamous famous for bad deeds

legend old story that might not be true, or a very famous person from history

livestock farm animals raised for meat, dairy, or other uses

Mexican Revolution time of fighting between the people of Mexico and its leaders

parole leaving prison early on the condition of good behaviour. Parole is set for a certain amount of time.

rustler thief who steals farm animals, usually horses or cattle

sentence punishment for a crime, usually a period of time to be spent in jail

tavern bar, pub, or inn

tyranny cruel leadership

Wild West western United States during the period of its settlement in the 1800s

Want to Know More?

Books

* *Highwaymen, Outlaws and Bandits of London*, Travis Elborough (Watling Street Ltd, 2004)
* *Robin Hood* (DK Read and Listen), Neil Philip (Dorling Kindersley, 2005)
* *True Crime: Outlaws*, John Townsend (Raintree, 2005)

Websites

* www.nedkellysworld.com.au
  Find out more about this Australian legend and other bushrangers.
* www.yahooligans.com
  Type "Robin Hood" or "Bonnie and Clyde" into this search engine and follow the links to find out more about these famous outlaws.

If you liked this Atomic book, why don't you try these...?

Index

Notes for adults

Use the following questions to guide children towards identifying features of recount text:

Can you find an example of a temporal connective on page 7?
Can you give an example of scene setting from page 11?
Can you find a recount of events on page 21?
Can you give examples of past tense language on page 25?
Can you give an example of a closing statement from page 28?